Good Meals for a Good Life

Meal Planner Notebook

@ Journals & Notebooks

Copyright 2016

All Rights reserved. No part of this book may be reproduced or used in any way or formor by any means whether electronic or mechanical, this means that you cannot recordor photocopy any material ideas or tips that are provided in this book.

meal planner

	Monday	Tuesday	Wednesday
BREAKFAST			
SNACK			
LUNCH			
SNACK			
DINNER			

Notes:

Meal Planner

	Thursday	Friday	Saturday
BREAKFAST			
SNACK			
LUNCH			
SNACK			
DINNER			

	Sunday
BREAKFAST	
SNACK	
LUNCH	
SNACK	
DINNER	

Meal Planner

	Monday	Tuesday	Wednesday
BREAKFAST			
SNACK			
LUNCH			
SNACK			
DINNER			

Notes:

meal Planner

	Thursday	Friday	Saturday
BREAKFAST			
SNACK			
LUNCH			
SNACK			
DINNER			

	Sunday
BREAKFAST	
SNACK	
LUNCH	
SNACK	
DINNER	

Meal Planner

	Monday	Tuesday	Wednesday
BREAKFAST			
SNACK			
LUNCH			
SNACK			
DINNER			

Notes:

Meal Planner

	Thursday	Friday	Saturday
BREAKFAST			
SNACK			
LUNCH			
SNACK			
DINNER			

	Sunday
BREAKFAST	
SNACK	
LUNCH	
SNACK	
DINNER	

MEAL PLANNER

	Monday	Tuesday	Wednesday
BREAKFAST			
SNACK			
LUNCH			
SNACK			
DINNER			

Notes:

meal planner

	Thursday	Friday	Saturday
BREAKFAST			
SNACK			
LUNCH			
SNACK			
DINNER			

	Sunday
BREAKFAST	
SNACK	
LUNCH	
SNACK	
DINNER	

Meal Planner

	Monday	Tuesday	Wednesday
BREAKFAST			
SNACK			
LUNCH			
SNACK			
DINNER			

Notes:

MEAL PLANNER

	Thursday	Friday	Saturday
BREAKFAST			
SNACK			
LUNCH			
SNACK			
DINNER			

	Sunday
BREAKFAST	
SNACK	
LUNCH	
SNACK	
DINNER	

Meal Planner

	Monday	Tuesday	Wednesday
BREAKFAST			
SNACK			
LUNCH			
SNACK			
DINNER			

Notes:

Meal Planner

	Thursday	Friday	Saturday
BREAKFAST			
SNACK			
LUNCH			
SNACK			
DINNER			

	Sunday
BREAKFAST	
SNACK	
LUNCH	
SNACK	
DINNER	

Meal Planner

	Monday	Tuesday	Wednesday
BREAKFAST			
SNACK			
LUNCH			
SNACK			
DINNER			

Notes:

MEAL PLANNER

	Thursday	Friday	Saturday
BREAKFAST			
SNACK			
LUNCH			
SNACK			
DINNER			

	Sunday
BREAKFAST	
SNACK	
LUNCH	
SNACK	
DINNER	

meal planner

	Monday	Tuesday	Wednesday
BREAKFAST			
SNACK			
LUNCH			
SNACK			
DINNER			

Notes:

Meal Planner

	Thursday	Friday	Saturday
BREAKFAST			
SNACK			
LUNCH			
SNACK			
DINNER			

	Sunday
BREAKFAST	
SNACK	
LUNCH	
SNACK	
DINNER	

MEAL PLANNER

	Monday	Tuesday	Wednesday
BREAKFAST			
SNACK			
LUNCH			
SNACK			
DINNER			

Notes:

MEAL PLANNER

	Thursday	Friday	Saturday
BREAKFAST			
SNACK			
LUNCH			
SNACK			
DINNER			

	Sunday
BREAKFAST	
SNACK	
LUNCH	
SNACK	
DINNER	

MEAL PLANNER

	Monday	Tuesday	Wednesday
BREAKFAST			
SNACK			
LUNCH			
SNACK			
DINNER			

Notes:

____

____

____

____

____

____

____

____

meal planner

	Thursday	Friday	Saturday
BREAKFAST			
SNACK			
LUNCH			
SNACK			
DINNER			

	Sunday
BREAKFAST	
SNACK	
LUNCH	
SNACK	
DINNER	

Meal Planner

	Monday	Tuesday	Wednesday
BREAKFAST			
SNACK			
LUNCH			
SNACK			
DINNER			

Notes:

MEAL PLANNER

	Thursday	Friday	Saturday
BREAKFAST			
SNACK			
LUNCH			
SNACK			
DINNER			

	Sunday
BREAKFAST	
SNACK	
LUNCH	
SNACK	
DINNER	

meal PLanner

	Monday	Tuesday	Wednesday
BREAKFAST			
SNACK			
LUNCH			
SNACK			
DINNER			

Notes:

Meal Planner

	Thursday	Friday	Saturday
BREAKFAST			
SNACK			
LUNCH			
SNACK			
DINNER			

	Sunday
BREAKFAST	
SNACK	
LUNCH	
SNACK	
DINNER	

Meal Planner

	Monday	Tuesday	Wednesday
BREAKFAST			
SNACK			
LUNCH			
SNACK			
DINNER			

Notes:

MEAL PLANNER

	Thursday	Friday	Saturday
BREAKFAST			
SNACK			
LUNCH			
SNACK			
DINNER			

	Sunday
BREAKFAST	
SNACK	
LUNCH	
SNACK	
DINNER	

Meal Planner

	Monday	Tuesday	Wednesday
BREAKFAST			
SNACK			
LUNCH			
SNACK			
DINNER			

Notes:

MEAL PLANNER

	Thursday	Friday	Saturday
BREAKFAST			
SNACK			
LUNCH			
SNACK			
DINNER			

	Sunday
BREAKFAST	
SNACK	
LUNCH	
SNACK	
DINNER	

MEAL PLANNER

	Monday	Tuesday	Wednesday
BREAKFAST			
SNACK			
LUNCH			
SNACK			
DINNER			

Notes:

Meal Planner

	Thursday	Friday	Saturday
BREAKFAST			
SNACK			
LUNCH			
SNACK			
DINNER			

	Sunday
BREAKFAST	
SNACK	
LUNCH	
SNACK	
DINNER	

Meal Planner

	Monday	Tuesday	Wednesday
BREAKFAST			
SNACK			
LUNCH			
SNACK			
DINNER			

Notes:

meal planner

	Thursday	Friday	Saturday
BREAKFAST			
SNACK			
LUNCH			
SNACK			
DINNER			

	Sunday
BREAKFAST	
SNACK	
LUNCH	
SNACK	
DINNER	

meal PLanneR

	Monday	Tuesday	Wednesday
BREAKFAST			
SNACK			
LUNCH			
SNACK			
DINNER			

Notes:

MEAL PLANNER

	Thursday	Friday	Saturday
BREAKFAST			
SNACK			
LUNCH			
SNACK			
DINNER			

	Sunday
BREAKFAST	
SNACK	
LUNCH	
SNACK	
DINNER	

meal planner

	Monday	Tuesday	Wednesday
BREAKFAST			
SNACK			
LUNCH			
SNACK			
DINNER			

Notes:

Meal Planner

	Thursday	Friday	Saturday
BREAKFAST			
SNACK			
LUNCH			
SNACK			
DINNER			

	Sunday
BREAKFAST	
SNACK	
LUNCH	
SNACK	
DINNER	

Meal Planner

	Monday	Tuesday	Wednesday
BREAKFAST			
SNACK			
LUNCH			
SNACK			
DINNER			

Notes:
____
____
____

____
____
____
____
____

MEAL PLANNER

	Thursday	Friday	Saturday
BREAKFAST			
SNACK			
LUNCH			
SNACK			
DINNER			

	Sunday
BREAKFAST	
SNACK	
LUNCH	
SNACK	
DINNER	

MEaL PLaNNER

	Monday	Tuesday	Wednesday
BREAKFAST			
SNACK			
LUNCH			
SNACK			
DINNER			

Notes:

Meal Planner

	Thursday	Friday	Saturday
BREAKFAST			
SNACK			
LUNCH			
SNACK			
DINNER			

	Sunday
BREAKFAST	
SNACK	
LUNCH	
SNACK	
DINNER	

meal planner

	Monday	Tuesday	Wednesday
BREAKFAST			
SNACK			
LUNCH			
SNACK			
DINNER			

Notes:

MEAL PLANNER

	Thursday	Friday	Saturday
BREAKFAST			
SNACK			
LUNCH			
SNACK			
DINNER			

	Sunday
BREAKFAST	
SNACK	
LUNCH	
SNACK	
DINNER	

meal Planner

	Monday	Tuesday	Wednesday
BREAKFAST			
SNACK			
LUNCH			
SNACK			
DINNER			

Notes:

____

____

____

____

____

____

____

____

MEAL PLANNER

	Thursday	Friday	Saturday
BREAKFAST			
SNACK			
LUNCH			
SNACK			
DINNER			

	Sunday
BREAKFAST	
SNACK	
LUNCH	
SNACK	
DINNER	

Meal Planner

	Monday	Tuesday	Wednesday
BREAKFAST			
SNACK			
LUNCH			
SNACK			
DINNER			

Notes:

____

____

____

____

____

____

____

Meal Planner

	Thursday	Friday	Saturday
BREAKFAST			
SNACK			
LUNCH			
SNACK			
DINNER			

	Sunday
BREAKFAST	
SNACK	
LUNCH	
SNACK	
DINNER	

Meal Planner

	Monday	Tuesday	Wednesday
BREAKFAST			
SNACK			
LUNCH			
SNACK			
DINNER			

Notes:

Meal Planner

	Thursday	Friday	Saturday
BREAKFAST			
SNACK			
LUNCH			
SNACK			
DINNER			

	Sunday
BREAKFAST	
SNACK	
LUNCH	
SNACK	
DINNER	

Meal Planner

	Monday	Tuesday	Wednesday
BREAKFAST			
SNACK			
LUNCH			
SNACK			
DINNER			

Notes:

Meal Planner

	Thursday	Friday	Saturday
BREAKFAST			
SNACK			
LUNCH			
SNACK			
DINNER			

	Sunday
BREAKFAST	
SNACK	
LUNCH	
SNACK	
DINNER	

MEAL PLANNER

	Monday	Tuesday	Wednesday
BREAKFAST			
SNACK			
LUNCH			
SNACK			
DINNER			

Notes:

MEAL PLANNER

	Thursday	Friday	Saturday
BREAKFAST			
SNACK			
LUNCH			
SNACK			
DINNER			

	Sunday
BREAKFAST	
SNACK	
LUNCH	
SNACK	
DINNER	

Meal Planner

	Monday	Tuesday	Wednesday
BREAKFAST			
SNACK			
LUNCH			
SNACK			
DINNER			

Notes:

Meal Planner

	Thursday	Friday	Saturday
BREAKFAST			
SNACK			
LUNCH			
SNACK			
DINNER			

	Sunday
BREAKFAST	
SNACK	
LUNCH	
SNACK	
DINNER	

Meal Planner

	Monday	Tuesday	Wednesday
BREAKFAST			
SNACK			
LUNCH			
SNACK			
DINNER			

Notes:

Meal Planner

	Thursday	Friday	Saturday
BREAKFAST			
SNACK			
LUNCH			
SNACK			
DINNER			

	Sunday
BREAKFAST	
SNACK	
LUNCH	
SNACK	
DINNER	

MEAL PLANNER

	Monday	Tuesday	Wednesday
BREAKFAST			
SNACK			
LUNCH			
SNACK			
DINNER			

Notes:

____

____

____

____

____

____

____

____

meal planner

	Thursday	Friday	Saturday
BREAKFAST			
SNACK			
LUNCH			
SNACK			
DINNER			

	Sunday
BREAKFAST	
SNACK	
LUNCH	
SNACK	
DINNER	

MEAL PLANNER

	Monday	Tuesday	Wednesday
BREAKFAST			
SNACK			
LUNCH			
SNACK			
DINNER			

Notes:

MEAL PLANNER

	Thursday	Friday	Saturday
BREAKFAST			
SNACK			
LUNCH			
SNACK			
DINNER			

	Sunday
BREAKFAST	
SNACK	
LUNCH	
SNACK	
DINNER	

Meal Planner

	Monday	Tuesday	Wednesday
BREAKFAST			
SNACK			
LUNCH			
SNACK			
DINNER			

Notes:

MeaL PLanneR

	Thursday	Friday	Saturday
BREAKFAST			
SNACK			
LUNCH			
SNACK			
DINNER			

	Sunday
BREAKFAST	
SNACK	
LUNCH	
SNACK	
DINNER	

meal planner

	Monday	Tuesday	Wednesday
BREAKFAST			
SNACK			
LUNCH			
SNACK			
DINNER			

Notes:

MEAL PLANNER

	Thursday	Friday	Saturday
BREAKFAST			
SNACK			
LUNCH			
SNACK			
DINNER			

	Sunday
BREAKFAST	
SNACK	
LUNCH	
SNACK	
DINNER	

Meal Planner

	Monday	Tuesday	Wednesday
BREAKFAST			
SNACK			
LUNCH			
SNACK			
DINNER			

Notes:

Meal Planner

	Thursday	Friday	Saturday
BREAKFAST			
SNACK			
LUNCH			
SNACK			
DINNER			

	Sunday
BREAKFAST	
SNACK	
LUNCH	
SNACK	
DINNER	

Meal Planner

	Monday	Tuesday	Wednesday
BREAKFAST			
SNACK			
LUNCH			
SNACK			
DINNER			

Notes:

MEAL PLANNER

	Thursday	Friday	Saturday
BREAKFAST			
SNACK			
LUNCH			
SNACK			
DINNER			

	Sunday
BREAKFAST	
SNACK	
LUNCH	
SNACK	
DINNER	

Meal Planner

	Monday	Tuesday	Wednesday
BREAKFAST			
SNACK			
LUNCH			
SNACK			
DINNER			

Notes:

MEAL PLANNER

	Thursday	Friday	Saturday
BREAKFAST			
SNACK			
LUNCH			
SNACK			
DINNER			

	Sunday
BREAKFAST	
SNACK	
LUNCH	
SNACK	
DINNER	

meal planner

	Monday	Tuesday	Wednesday
BREAKFAST			
SNACK			
LUNCH			
SNACK			
DINNER			

Notes:

MeaL PLanNeR

	Thursday	Friday	Saturday
BREAKFAST			
SNACK			
LUNCH			
SNACK			
DINNER			

	Sunday
BREAKFAST	
SNACK	
LUNCH	
SNACK	
DINNER	

meal planner

	Monday	Tuesday	Wednesday
BREAKFAST			
SNACK			
LUNCH			
SNACK			
DINNER			

Notes:

Meal Planner

	Thursday	Friday	Saturday
BREAKFAST			
SNACK			
LUNCH			
SNACK			
DINNER			

	Sunday
BREAKFAST	
SNACK	
LUNCH	
SNACK	
DINNER	

MEAL PLANNER

	Monday	Tuesday	Wednesday
BREAKFAST			
SNACK			
LUNCH			
SNACK			
DINNER			

Notes:

MEAL PLANNER

	Thursday	Friday	Saturday
BREAKFAST			
SNACK			
LUNCH			
SNACK			
DINNER			

	Sunday
BREAKFAST	
SNACK	
LUNCH	
SNACK	
DINNER	

MEAL PLANNER

	Monday	Tuesday	Wednesday
BREAKFAST			
SNACK			
LUNCH			
SNACK			
DINNER			

Notes:

meaL PLanneR

	Thursday	Friday	Saturday
BREAKFAST			
SNACK			
LUNCH			
SNACK			
DINNER			

	Sunday
BREAKFAST	
SNACK	
LUNCH	
SNACK	
DINNER	

Meal Planner

	Monday	Tuesday	Wednesday
BREAKFAST			
SNACK			
LUNCH			
SNACK			
DINNER			

Notes:

Meal Planner

	Thursday	Friday	Saturday
BREAKFAST			
SNACK			
LUNCH			
SNACK			
DINNER			

	Sunday
BREAKFAST	
SNACK	
LUNCH	
SNACK	
DINNER	

MEAL PLANNER

	Monday	Tuesday	Wednesday
BREAKFAST			
SNACK			
LUNCH			
SNACK			
DINNER			

Notes:

MEAL PLANNER

	Thursday	Friday	Saturday
BREAKFAST			
SNACK			
LUNCH			
SNACK			
DINNER			

	Sunday
BREAKFAST	
SNACK	
LUNCH	
SNACK	
DINNER	

meal Planner

	Monday	Tuesday	Wednesday
BREAKFAST			
SNACK			
LUNCH			
SNACK			
DINNER			

Notes:

MEAL PLANNER

	Thursday	Friday	Saturday
BREAKFAST			
SNACK			
LUNCH			
SNACK			
DINNER			

	Sunday
BREAKFAST	
SNACK	
LUNCH	
SNACK	
DINNER	

meal planner

	Monday	Tuesday	Wednesday
BREAKFAST			
SNACK			
LUNCH			
SNACK			
DINNER			

Notes:

MEAL PLANNER

	Thursday	Friday	Saturday
BREAKFAST			
SNACK			
LUNCH			
SNACK			
DINNER			

	Sunday
BREAKFAST	
SNACK	
LUNCH	
SNACK	
DINNER	

MEAL PLANNER

	Monday	Tuesday	Wednesday
BREAKFAST			
SNACK			
LUNCH			
SNACK			
DINNER			

Notes:

Meal Planner

	Thursday	Friday	Saturday
BREAKFAST			
SNACK			
LUNCH			
SNACK			
DINNER			

	Sunday
BREAKFAST	
SNACK	
LUNCH	
SNACK	
DINNER	

Meal Planner

	Monday	Tuesday	Wednesday
BREAKFAST			
SNACK			
LUNCH			
SNACK			
DINNER			

Notes:

Meal Planner

	Thursday	Friday	Saturday
BREAKFAST			
SNACK			
LUNCH			
SNACK			
DINNER			

	Sunday
BREAKFAST	
SNACK	
LUNCH	
SNACK	
DINNER	

meal planner

	Monday	Tuesday	Wednesday
BREAKFAST			
SNACK			
LUNCH			
SNACK			
DINNER			

Notes:

MEAL PLANNER

	Thursday	Friday	Saturday
BREAKFAST			
SNACK			
LUNCH			
SNACK			
DINNER			

	Sunday
BREAKFAST	
SNACK	
LUNCH	
SNACK	
DINNER	

Meal Planner

	Monday	Tuesday	Wednesday
BREAKFAST			
SNACK			
LUNCH			
SNACK			
DINNER			

Notes:

Meal Planner

	Thursday	Friday	Saturday
BREAKFAST			
SNACK			
LUNCH			
SNACK			
DINNER			

	Sunday
BREAKFAST	
SNACK	
LUNCH	
SNACK	
DINNER	

MEAL PLANNER

	Monday	Tuesday	Wednesday
BREAKFAST			
SNACK			
LUNCH			
SNACK			
DINNER			

Notes:
____
____
____
____
____
____
____
____

meal planner

	Thursday	Friday	Saturday
BREAKFAST			
SNACK			
LUNCH			
SNACK			
DINNER			

	Sunday
BREAKFAST	
SNACK	
LUNCH	
SNACK	
DINNER	

MEAL PLANNER

	Monday	Tuesday	Wednesday
BREAKFAST			
SNACK			
LUNCH			
SNACK			
DINNER			

Notes:

meal planner

	Thursday	Friday	Saturday
BREAKFAST			
SNACK			
LUNCH			
SNACK			
DINNER			

	Sunday
BREAKFAST	
SNACK	
LUNCH	
SNACK	
DINNER	

Meal Planner

	Monday	Tuesday	Wednesday
BREAKFAST			
SNACK			
LUNCH			
SNACK			
DINNER			

Notes:

Meal Planner

	Thursday	Friday	Saturday
BREAKFAST			
SNACK			
LUNCH			
SNACK			
DINNER			

	Sunday
BREAKFAST	
SNACK	
LUNCH	
SNACK	
DINNER	

MEAL PLANNER

	Monday	Tuesday	Wednesday
BREAKFAST			
SNACK			
LUNCH			
SNACK			
DINNER			

Notes:

MEAL PLANNER

	Thursday	Friday	Saturday
BREAKFAST			
SNACK			
LUNCH			
SNACK			
DINNER			

	Sunday
BREAKFAST	
SNACK	
LUNCH	
SNACK	
DINNER	

Meal Planner

	Monday	Tuesday	Wednesday
BREAKFAST			
SNACK			
LUNCH			
SNACK			
DINNER			

Notes:

MEAL PLANNER

	Thursday	Friday	Saturday
BREAKFAST			
SNACK			
LUNCH			
SNACK			
DINNER			

	Sunday
BREAKFAST	
SNACK	
LUNCH	
SNACK	
DINNER	

www.ingramcontent.com/pod-product-compliance
Lightning Source LLC
Chambersburg PA
CBHW081311250726

48662CB00008B/2505